10 STEPS TO A CAPSULE WARDROBE

How to look great, feel confident & save time with a capsule wardrobe

LISA TALBOT

LISA TALBOT
PERSONAL STYLIST

Contents

AUTHOR BIO

Lisa Talbot is a fully qualified Personal and Fashion stylist. Lisa trained initially as an Image consultant and also with the *'London College of Style'* enhancing her Personal Styling skills. Lisa is an Award Winning personal & fashion stylist and she is passionate about helping both ladies and gentlemen dress for their personality, lifestyle and body shape. Lisa also helps people to re-organise their wardrobes to focus on essential items of clothing and styles which suit her clients and allow them to always feel confident and look great.

Lisa has featured on radio, appeared on a number of television shows and written style comment for numerous publications. Lisa presents at a number of events where her informal, natural approach is loved by many.

In this book Lisa explains the steps needed to simplify your wardrobes and ensure that we always have a mix of complementary clothing. Having a Capsule Wardrobe makes life so much easier.

Lisa is practically minded and always focuses on helping people have a wardrobe that they love and want to wear.

TESTIMONIALS

"Thank you for a brilliant virtual Wardrobe consultation, I was skeptical but I really enjoyed it and the way you have refreshed my outfit choices is great"

\

"To be honest (I'll say it again!) I would never have picked out or tried any of the items myself but I'm glad I trusted your expertise and let you push me out of my comfort zone. I feel like my wardrobe has been completely refreshed and has had a much needed injection of "zing"! There are so many different combinations and it feels fun and young, but still classy. Thank you so much Lisa for your patience and incredible advice"

"I've just opened up my goodies from yesterday and it feels like Christmas! Thank you for spending time with me and pushing me out of my comfort zone. I feel that I will be able to shop more confidently for my size and shape with the direction you offered."

"Really enjoyed wardrobe consultation and how you put together outfits I would not of thought of. Also had a good clear out of my wardrobe and got rid of things I knew did nothing for me but just hung onto for no particular reason.

"Didn't realise I had so many nice things and now all colour co-ordinated in my wardrobe, looks very impressive when you open it up."

"I've thoroughly enjoyed it. It's been like shopping in my own wardrobe"

INTRODUCTION

The experience from my professional career taught me that I loved being around people; I love getting to know their personalities and I have always had a love of clothes as well.

I concentrated on family commitments for some two and a half years. Once the children started attending Pre-school I then began a business selling children's clothing from my home. This was very successful so I extended the range to include a ladies collection. As I was doing this I found that I was talking to my customers more and giving them style and fashion advice, especially matching them with clothing which would suit them. I enjoyed doing this but felt I should take some training to be even better at it.

I learned about image consultancy, studied the effects of colours, how to dress different body shapes, how to put together a fashion wardrobe and I have also learned about personal shopping. I have then added my own personality to what I do and my business.

I learned how to give advice and information to my clients about their shapes, styles and colours to match them with the correct clothing. My home selling clothing business became much more informative and less about selling. I decided to set up a personal fashion stylist business to run alongside my sales business and to see how it went. I never dreamed of the success that followed!

I set my business up in 2012 and I now help both men and women from age 15 up to age 80 or so, and from all walks of life. Fashion and style has no age limit and believe it or not, it also has no money limit. Marvellous styles and looks can be achieved with any budget.

I took a second training course at the London College of Style which focused on styling and which allows me to do editorial photo shoots and to work with the media.

I work with several shopping centres for their style events and provide editorials for the media as well as working with lovely clients which is my passion.

I provide consultations that are bespoke and totally personal. I tailor my style consultations to suit each individual client so the advice they receive is relevant to them and only them. My services as a stylist are not out of reach financially for anybody because we can tailor consultations to suit everybody. People might think that taking advice from a fashion stylist has to be very expensive, but that is not true.

I now have a team of stylists based all over the UK, so we can help people up and down the country with clothing consultations and with putting together their capsule wardrobe.

In the usual course of events I am contacted by a prospective client by email with an enquiry. I provide them with information on the set of consultations that I offer and then I phone them up a few days later as I feel it is nice to speak to somebody personally and it also helps me better understand their requirements. I will ask the prospective customer some questions. I might ask them what they are struggling with at the moment or what they find really easy with regards to their clothing. Some customers might say that they work five days a week and that they have a uniform for their work but that they struggle with their casual clothes at the weekend. I will then ask them what they do for a job, what their family situation is and begin to build a picture of the person to help me advise them on the range of clothing which might be suitable for them. I always keep in mind that I am helping my clients get what they want and not what I think they want, so it is important that we work together. We therefore work as a kind of partnership and it is never about me telling my customer what they are going to do or what they are going to wear, but rather about me giving them the expert advice on how they can get the most out of their clothing to suit their body shape, their colour, their style preferences and their purse. We work together.

I like to help educate and teach my customers what they should look out for when they are shopping online or in the shops and to know what will work for them and what won't, what colour is good for them and what is not. This educational process is great fun.

I also offer an after-care service so I always follow-up with my clients to ask how they are getting on. A growing number of my customers come back to me for more clothing advice and it is great to stay in touch with them.

My services include *'Wardrobe Consultations'* and *'Personal shopping'* as well as *'Colours'* and *'How to dress your body shape'*. I now have a consultation called *'The Online Wardrobe'*, Fall back in love with old favourites. Discover brands new looks hand-picked just for you. The Online Wardrobe is a personal styling consultation with a twist and is available as a App.

From items in your existing wardrobe to new finds, I create custom outfits to suit your personality, lifestyle and body shape – all on the revolutionary online styling platform

I hope you enjoy reading my book. If you should need help or advice I would be delighted to hear from you.

Lots of love
Lisa xx

| STEP 1 |

WHAT IS A CAPSULE WARDROBE?

A Capsule Wardrobe is a small collection of clothes you love!
Have you ever been abroad, perhaps in France or Italy, and seen the local people in cities walking around looking very smart and well dressed? They may have clothes that co-ordinate well, and all finished off with an accessory such as a scarf, costume jewellery or a handbag. They often look like they have spent a lot on their clothes. Believe it or not, many Europeans do not spend a great deal on clothes. They don't buy many clothes, but what they buy is of the best quality they can afford, and they ensure it goes with the other clothes they own. And they mix them up and wear different things together at different times. Such people have learned the essence of a *'capsule wardrobe!'*

A capsule wardrobe is a normal wardrobe of any shape or size but which has items of clothing in it which can all interlink to create numerous outfits. For example, a capsule wardrobe may contain 15 items of clothing that can all be interchanged so that it can create perhaps 30 different outfits. The wardrobe itself and the range of clothing in it need not be great, in fact they are usually quite small, yet they can be used to create many different looks and styles when mixed and matched together. This means that by buying a small number of suitable items of clothing a person can create a whole range of possible looks and get the most for their money. There are, however, considerations to the styles and types of clothing because essentially all or most should be interchangeable with other items of clothing in the wardrobe.

To begin with there should be a set of what we call base neutral colours which are usually in block colours and which might be black, navy, brown, green or beige. Then there can be some print items, but they should all interlink. For ladies there should be a jacket and perhaps some dresses, but all taken together you create a wardrobe that works for the person's personality, their lifestyle and their body shape.

A good capsule wardrobe will allow a lady or gentleman to get up in the morning and know that they could wear any of the trousers with any tops or jackets. Then the following day they can perhaps wear the same top but they could mix it with a skirt and a cardigan which all go together. Then the following day they might wear a dress which mixes well with the cardigan and a different pair of shoes.

In this way it makes the person's life much easier and more cost effective, there is less clutter, and it takes up much less room.

I know some people who go out and buy their menfolk a set of clothes for a season which will last them for the season and they do not buy anything else in between seasons. Alternatively, people with a capsule wardrobe can know what style of clothing will fit into the capsule wardrobe well and can look out for suitable items of clothing if they need them and which they know will go with their other clothes (or at least most of them). In this way, pieces can be added to the capsule wardrobe but always in coordination with the other items in it. For instance, a lady might be out shopping and see a yellow print top and she will know that it will go well with the navy trousers she has in her capsule wardrobe. Each item of clothing becomes an interlink between the others.

A man might have three pairs of trousers, these being grey, navy and black. He may have a range of shirts which might have different block colours, block white or stripes, but they will all interlink with the trousers. This keeps the look modern, fresh and stylish, but in an easy way and it allows the wardrobe to be worn all the time.

Many of us have a wardrobe which is bulging full but we only wear perhaps 20% of the clothes in it for at least 80% of the time. A capsule wardrobe allows every item of clothing to be worn in the knowledge that it will mix easily with other items of clothing so that the whole wardrobe is used regularly. The net effect is that although the person may actually own far fewer items of clothing, their look and style is far more varied because they are wearing all of it rather than just 20% of the wardrobe for most of the time.

One aim of the capsule wardrobe is to have items of clothing which go together and can be worn with other items of clothing. It is possible to have clothes at either end of the spectrum that shouldn't be worn together, but they should be able to be worn with enough items of clothing in the capsule wardrobe to be able to make several outfits. The majority of clothes should therefore compliment each other. A person might have a cardigan that will go with a dress and a blazer that goes with trousers, but they might have a yellow shirt that does not go with printed trousers. So long as they are not worn together it is okay as they can be worn with many other items of clothing in the capsule wardrobe.

Capsule wardrobes therefore save room and are less cluttered they certainly do not have to be boring. They allow us to have coordinated clothes that we can easily see, and which we wear. They make our lives easier because it will never be a struggle to know what goes with what. They help us always look our best, and they can save us money. So how do we go about making a capsule wardrobe in the first place? That's the next step.

HOW DO I DRESS FOR LESS AND LOOK GREAT?

'My mission in life is not merely to survive, but to thrive;
and to do so with some passion, some compassion, some
humour, and some style."
Maya Angelou

The whole idea and basis of having a capsule wardrobe is to make sure that you get great value for money. When we talk about dressing for less and still looking great, we are not necessarily saying we should buy lots of cheap items of clothing, but rather it is about working out your budget and then getting the most from it.

Setting a budget for clothing is not something that many of us do. It is a good place to start, however. Whether we set a budget or not, we all have a budget for clothing. If we add up over a year what we spend on clothing we can then divide that by 12 and it shall give us a rough figure on what our budget for clothes has been each month. Unless it was an exceptional year this can set a notional budget for the future. The important thing is to have some idea of what the budget is. I therefore recommend that you think about this and work out what your monthly or bi-monthly budget for clothing might be. Alternatively, you might have a small amount as a lump sum available for clothes, perhaps following a birthday. That lump sum can then be your budget. The important thing is getting the best value for money with your budget.

Most of us want to try to look modern, fresh and stylish, but not necessarily overly trendy. We don't want to look old before our time but rather we would rather look age-appropriate while keeping things as young and modern, stylish and chic and as simple as possible. With the budget we have we can then identify the items of clothing that we might want to get longevity from. If we want an item of clothing to last a long time because it perhaps has a classic and rather timeless quality, then we want to buy the best quality item of clothing that our budget will allow. For instance, say you have decided that you can afford two items of clothing that you want to last for quite a while and one of them is a pair of jeans, you should look to spend a reasonable amount of money for a good quality pair of jeans which will last longer. The same goes if you are looking to buy a pair of shoes or a coat which you intend to keep for some time. There is a good saying which goes 'buy cheap, buy twice'. Cheaper items often wear out quicker because the quality is just not there. If you want the item of clothing to last a long time it is a false economy to buy cheaply.

Once you have items of clothing that are going to last longer and which perhaps are of better quality and which will see you through the season and into next year then you can add lesser priced items on a seasonal basis. This allows you to maintain a core of good quality clothes and use the balance of your budget to inject the key modern pieces of clothing to see you through. You will also not be wasting your money on items of clothing that you know you're not going to wear. Doing this you will always look great because you are going to look stylish and up-to-date but you're not going to have loads of unused clothing that used to cost you £10 or less and is of poor quality.

People sometimes think that if they have £100 to spend on clothing they want as many items as possible for that money. A better approach is to think about what you wear a lot of and then invest as much as you can for it. Some people might not think twice about spending £150 on a pair of jeans whereas for other people £40 is a lot for a pair of jeans. Whatever your budget is you just spend as much you can afford for the key items of clothing, and then you can spend a little less on the more seasonal clothes.

We now know what a capsule wardrobe is and the theory behind it. Putting it into practice can seem a little overwhelming, but you take it one step at a time. Getting started is the key and that is what we look at next.

| STEP 3 |

WHERE DO I START?

It's important to find what really suits who you are, because style isn't only what you wear, it's what you project.

Carolina Herrera

The best place to start is not down at the shops but rather at your wardrobe. Be prepared that this will take a little time so make sure you have an hour or more available before you attempt this. You want to be able to take time and not rush. I say to my clients that if 'they fail to plan then they plan to fail' and you do not want to be interrupted halfway through sorting out your wardrobe. Therefore plan to do it on a day when you know you have a little bit of time you can set aside.

First of all, when you are looking at your wardrobe, begin by turning all of the hangers the same way round. Often they are put back in the wardrobe about-face so get them all facing the same direction.

The next step is to go through each item of clothing. When you come across an item of clothing that you haven't worn for that season take the hanger out and hang it back in the wardrobe facing the opposite way. Straight away this will show you what clothes you wear regularly or occasionally and what clothes you haven't worn at all that season.

The next step is to look at the items of clothing that you have hung up the opposite way indicating that you have not worn them that season. Ask yourself whether you haven't worn them because it has been the wrong season i.e. they are maybe winter clothes and it is currently summer, or if it is because you simply haven't worn it. There are several reasons why we have clothes in our wardrobes that we don't wear. These reasons could be because they don't fit us anymore; it could be because we don't actually like them anymore; it could be because we had actually forgotten we had the item of clothing (especially if our wardrobe is overflowing!)

Once you have identified the items of clothing that you haven't worn (and it has nothing to do with the season) you have identified the clothes that you are going to take out of the wardrobe. Remember, if you are not wearing them then there is no point them cluttering up your wardrobe and you will feel a lot better if they are out of it!

There are various ways you can discard clothes from your wardrobe. You could set up a pile to donate to charity shops or collections. There are also second-hand shops that accept clothing. If it is a branded piece of clothing in good condition you might even be able to sell it, perhaps on an online auction site and get a little bit of money back towards buying new clothes. Or you can simply put unwanted clothes in the bin if you feel they cannot be re-purposed.

You can set up three or four piles depending on what destinations your clothes are going to. You then start going through the clothes you haven't been wearing and discard the clothes into whichever pile you decide they are going to. You will probably surprise yourself with how many new clothes you find which you have simply never worn.

If you come across clothes which perhaps don't fit you but you would like to wear them again, I would recommend you take them out of your wardrobe anyway so they don't clutter up the wardrobe, and store them under your bed or in the loft (if you have one). However, if you still don't wear them over the next year then I would recommend you remove.

While the above steps all look very easy I fully appreciate that for some people going through their wardrobe and throwing away their clothes or giving them to charity is not at all easy. This is one reason why I have many clients who ask me to help them do it with them! You can do it though. The process does take a little bit of courage and you have to prepare yourself and steel yourself for the task but trust me, it is worth it, and you will be glad you did it.

Next I shall give you some tips on how to choose what clothes to discard.

| STEP 4 |

WHAT CLOTHES SHOULD I GET RID OF?

"Fit is everything. I don't care what your body type is like:
If you're not wearing clothes that fit you,
you can't have style."
Stacy London

"The biggest criticism would be buying clothes that are too
big or trying too hard. I tend to like things a little leaner and
more formfitting. I believe personal style often
outweighs fashion. Just be yourself."
Simon Spurr

A large element of my *'Wardrobe Consultations'* actually consist of being more of a hand holder for my clients to give them strength and encouragement when they are looking through their wardrobes. It is sometimes easier for a third party to be involved because they do not have any personal connections to the clothing and we can be more matter-of-fact. This really does help sometimes.

It can be difficult to move things out of your wardrobe if you originally paid a lot of money for the item. The fact is though, if you do not wear it for whatever reason, it is simply wasting your space. Hopefully, when you implement the practices in this book you will find that you very seldom make unwise clothing purchases in future because you will know better what to look for and you will be less likely to impulse buy an item of clothing that you will never wear. So take some positives. You are learning!

Sometimes during *'Wardrobe Consultations'* I will take out an item of clothing and my client will automatically say they want to get rid of it without any prompting from me. For such items the decision is easy and there is no problem.

Many other items are harder to decide whether to discard or not.

- Ask yourself do you LOVE the piece?
- Ask yourself whether you have worn the item in the last couple of years?
- Ask yourself if it still fits you?
- Ask yourself if you would feel comfortable wearing the item of clothing?
- Ask yourself if you would feel good wearing the item of clothing?

If the answer to any of the above questions is **no** then you really should get rid of the item.

You might have a pair of trousers that you think look really nice but they are so uncomfortable that you never wear them. What's the point of keeping them?

If you have items that don't fit, maybe due to weight loss, weight gain or a change of shape it is, in my opinion, no point of these clothes being in your wardrobe. In fact, keeping them will be counter-productive. They create a very negative feel to your wardrobe and every time you open it. I would rather you have items in your wardrobe that you love and enjoy wearing.

Let's concentrate on what you **can** wear so you look and feel as fantastic as possible. Don't dwell on the past. Your future is looking good! Whatever money you have set yourself in your budget, so you can tell yourself that you are going to go shopping to replace some of the items. You know you will be building it back up, but this time with clothes that fit you well and make you feel more confident, stronger in your personality and ready to take on the world. Looking good and feeling great in clothes is all about getting a perfect fit, so if it doesn't fit perfectly then move it out! Get some positivity in your wardrobe!

Imagine the positive boost you will get each morning when you open your wardrobe and can only see clothes that you know fit you well and you look good in. Deciding what to wear will no longer be an agony or a cause for disappointment anymore, and you will have so much choice!

When you do shop, whether it be in store or online, bear in mind that different retailers cut the clothing to different sizes even if the labels say the same thing. I would always recommend that you try on new clothes to ensure that it is the perfect fit. Unless you are seriously embarking on a weight loss or weight gain plan, I strongly wouldn't recommend you buy clothes that you hope to be able to fit in, in the future. Live in the now and buy clothes that fit you now so you have clothes that you look good in now. If you were trying to lose or gain weight and managed to do so then you may need to buy some new sized clothes but that shall be a reward for you in future; a delicious carrot to reward yourself with rather than a stick to put in your wardrobe to beat yourself up with. Beware however, that clothes that are size 12 in one shop might actually be a size 16 in another shop. Don't go by what the label says, it is only a rough guide.

The style of the item of clothing will also influence the sizing. When boxy jumpers are more in fashion (which they are at present) for ladies, it is usually possible to go down a size because the garments are quite spacious. Conversely, with men's shirts at the moment, they often have a very narrow cut especially with certain brands such as Ted Baker, so men will often not fit into the usual shirts sizing. Other brands such as Gant for Men have more of a straight cut and are quite roomy. Different brands and different shops will therefore have different sizings. As a result certain retailers and brands can suit people's body shape better than others. I'm often helping my clients to educate them on which shops and which brands they will be best off looking at because of their particular shape.

Occasionally we have treasured memories which are invoked by certain items of clothing. Seeing the clothing may bring back the memory and this might make it very difficult to throw the piece of clothing away even though you never wear it any more. If that is the case it is still not right to keep the wardrobe cluttered with clothes you don't wear, so I would recommend that you put the item of clothing in a vacuum pack and keep it somewhere else. It is a bit like ladies keeping their wedding dresses purely for the memory. There is nothing wrong with that. I had a client whose husband had passed away. He used to buy her Disney character fleeces when he went to America. She told me she never wore them but didn't want to get rid of them because of their special meaning. I advised her to pack them away safely as a keepsake. We can keep our memories but we do not want them to impinge on what we are doing on a daily basis.

Okay, now we have a wardrobe that is looking tidier, organised and leaner. Now we might want to add a few items of clothing to it, but we are constrained by our budget. So how do we go about shopping on our budget? That is the next step.

| STEP 5 |

SHOPPING ON YOUR BUDGET

"Buy Less, Choose Well"
Vivienne Westwood

"I think of each new season as an evolution,
not a change in style."
Manolo Blahnik

First of all before you go shopping (and before every Personal Shopping Consultation I do with my clients) you should always look in your wardrobe to see what you actually need. A key part of shopping on a budget is actually simply to buy **only what you need** and what you know is going to interlink back into your wardrobe and go well with the items of clothing you have kept and will be wearing. Shopping should therefore not be a random process and you should have in mind a clear type of clothing and fashion before you take your purse or wallet anywhere near the shops. If you take away all the random purchases (which often don't go well with other clothes) you will save money in your budget which you can then channel towards either better quality clothes or the interlinking seasonal clothes that you need.

Take five minutes to look in your wardrobe to remind yourself what clothes you have there to give you some idea of what you will need. Maybe you could do with a new pair of trousers? By looking at your wardrobe you will have an idea of what colour or print the trousers can be to interlink with the other clothes in your thinned out wardrobe. You can also look through your tops to ensure that the intended colour or design you want to buy will fit in with them. If you store tops in drawers rather than in your wardrobe then you should apply the same process to the drawers as you do for your wardrobe. Although we refer to it being a capsule wardrobe the term *'wardrobe'* covers **all of your clothing storage units.** In for a penny in for a pound. If you are going to do this, do it across the board!

Once you have refreshed your memory on what clothes you have in your wardrobe and an idea of what you need, then you look at your budget. Everybody's budget is different and none are right and none are wrong.

The Online Wardrobe that I offer has the ability for a client to upload their wardrobe to a mobile App so you can take your wardrobe shopping with you, how fantastic is that? https://www.lisatalbot.co.uk/the-online-wardrobe/

Some of my clients, for instance, say they have a monthly budget of £30 to spend, but it could be less. Others tell me that they have a lump sum of £300 to spend. With the amazing High Street & Online retailers as it is there is a huge range of clothing and prices so that pretty much any budget can be catered for. All the budget does is sometimes dictate where you can shop. Your budget may decide for you whether you can afford to shop in the general shops in the High Street or seek out a middle brand, a top brand or even a designer brand. Obviously you may have your own views about whether designer brands are worth the money they charge or even whether you like them. They are not everyone's cup of tea. In any event your budget will tell you broadly what level of expense and what level of brand you can look for.

It is important to set the budget before you go shopping
Once you have organised your wardrobe and know what clothes you need, and once you have set your budget, you will not feel that you are wasting money when you go clothes shopping because you will have assigned the money for it and know you need the clothes. You should not get *'buyer's remorse'* and feelings of guilt from shopping in this way, but you should be very pleased when you find items which you know will fit in with your capsule wardrobe. Is also very unlikely that you will make an impulse buy for an item of clothing which you are unlikely to wear. You will be a lot more disciplined in your approach, and that will save you money and help you to keep in budget.

One month you might realise that the season is changing and you could do with a new pair of shoes rather than buy any clothes. Or you might think that it is time to buy an accessory such as a necklace which will give a different look to some of the tops that you wear.

It is about making sure that whatever you buy works for your wardrobe and sometimes it is not actually clothes that you need, but accessories. Accessories, especially for ladies, can really liven up and change the look of their outfits and so are a great way of keeping their look fresh and fashionable.

Using the seasons **'on trend'** colour is a great way to inject the modern look to your outfit. Ladies might have a white shirt in her wardrobe and a very nice pair of jeans that they feel comfortable in, they might not want any clothing that is the on trend colour but want to look up-to-date, they then have the option of buying an accessory in this colour. This keeps the whole outfit up-to-date and rather trendy. The accessory will work with their wardrobe. Don't get hung up with your budget as you will be able to achieve what you want just so long as you make sure it works for you and your wardrobe.

As you can probably see it is very much about being a little more **disciplined**. It is about knowing what you need by looking in your wardrobe before you go shopping. It is about setting a budget and sticking to it by finding the shops and the brands which fall within your budget. It is about not drifting off and looking at clothes you don't need or that will not work with your wardrobe and it is about not making impulse buys that you will never wear. Trust me, you will thank yourself for doing this!

Another aspect you need to keep in mind is to ensure that any new clothes you buy fit in with your lifestyle. You might see a dress that you love but if you never go to places where you would wear such a dress then clearly you will be wasting your money if you bought it on impulse just because it looked nice. A full-time mum may not go out as much as a single lady and so not wear a formal dress from one year to another. However, if they know they have a function coming up, such as a wedding, then they can shop for appropriate clothes within their budget and buy in the knowledge that it should still work with their wardrobe for when the next function arises.

Have the discipline to stop yourself before you make a purchase and ask if the item of clothing would work with the rest of your wardrobe. If the answer is yes and it also works for your budget and lifestyle, then go for it!

Now we know what types of clothes to buy and what budget we are working with. How do we ensure that our wardrobe does not become as cluttered as it was previously? The guide to this is contained in the next step.

| STEP 6 |

HOW MANY CLOTHES SHOULD I HAVE?

Simplicity in character, in manners, in style;
in all things the supreme excellence is simplicity.
Henry Wadsworth Longfellow

As a rule of thumb we say that if you have 15 items of clothing per season you should be able to create more than 30 outfits by mixing them up. When I say items of clothing I do not mean shoes but rather the fabric items such as trousers, skirts, dresses, blazers, coats, blouses and so forth. On this basis, if I were advising a lady, I would be recommending that she have around 15 items of clothing per season, all as high quality as possible and most of them being able to go well with other items. I would recommend that a lady has, say, three dresses. These could be stand-alone items of clothing. If the lady doesn't work then they could be casual dresses or more formal if the lady goes to work. She could then have perhaps two skirts, four pairs of trousers and then the remainder is made up of tops. The tops should interlink and go with the bottoms. The number of dresses compared to trousers and skirts can vary depending upon the lady's preference and lifestyle. Some ladies never wear a skirt so she might have more tops or more trousers.

Although it seems a remarkably low number, 15 items of clothing per season is the amount I recommend as it really is all a person needs. In my opinion and experience 15 is the optimum number, not the minimum. Remember, you are trying to build a smaller capsule wardrobe that works for more occasions and where everything is easily seen and gets worn. There are no hidden nooks and crannies where old items of clothing reside which you never wear. Everything is efficient and in use. With these 15 items you can create well over 30 mix-and-match outfits, so there is very little risk of ever appearing the same when you go out. On this point just bear in mind that someone with a very disorganised and cluttered wardrobe is only likely to ever be wearing at most 20% of the clothes they have, which will usually be the ones that they can see or get to in the cluttered wardrobe. Once the wardrobe is thinned out and has only 15 items in it they can all be seen and accessed so easily that every day can be different.

Again if this seems difficult, think of it this way; when you go on holiday and especially if you go abroad, you have to sometimes pack two weeks' worth of clothing into one suitcase. You never take the whole of your wardrobe, only clothes that you need for those two weeks. You take some items for the beach if it is a beach holiday and you take some items for the evening. Because you are so restricted with your baggage allowance you take things that you know will go with the other items so you can mix and match clothes over the two weeks. Having a capsule wardrobe is very much like this. You choose carefully what goes in the suitcase (and the capsule wardrobe) and you know that what is in it will go with everything else (pretty much). Having a capsule wardrobe is almost like thinking it is suitcase and that you are going on a long holiday, and you make the fabrics work.

One aspect of packing a suitcase for a holiday is that as you are only going for two weeks it is likely that you will encounter only one type of seasonal weather and so you pack accordingly. Similarly with a capsule wardrobe when I say 15 items of clothing I mean 15 items that are suited to the current season, and when I refer to the season I actually mean summer and winter. In other words for clothing seasons there are two in each year. I recommend to my clients that they have 15 items of clothing for the summer season and 15 items of clothing for the winter season. Obviously these clothes are rotated depending upon season. Some of my clients will store away the previous season's clothes to make space in their capsule wardrobe. However, some items of clothing which are intended for the summer season can actually be worn in the winter season perhaps underneath as another layer. T-shirts and shirts, for instance, can often be worn summer or winter, only that in winter they form a base layer.

Taking into account the two seasons of each year and having 15 items of clothing suited to each season, the total number of fabric items of clothing is 30. An example of the contents of a typical capsule wardrobe for men and women are shown below:-

15 items for Women	15 items for Men
4 x Bottoms	5 x Bottoms
1 x Dress	9 x Tops
9 x Tops	1 x Coat
1 x Coat	= 15
= 15	

If you are wondering if I practice what I preach I can confirm that my own wardrobe has got precisely 15 items of clothing in it. I move older items out and bring new items in each season. The budget I work to is seasonal and each season is £400. I don't expect to pay a King's ransom for good quality clothes which suit me. At £400 per season I am budgeting to spend roughly £800 per year on clothes. This works out to be just under £70 per month as a budget.

To keep to my quite modest budget I learnt to smart shop. If I saw an item of clothing I needed, for instance in Top Shop, but which cost £65, I would decide whether I was prepared to pay £65 for it and if not I would take a chance and wait for the sales. Recently I did just this and instead of paying £65 I managed to pick it up in a sale for £20. Result!

The important aspect of my above example is that I had pre-planned what clothes I wanted to buy and was specifically looking out for them in the sale. The problem with shopping in sales is that it is very tempting to buy random items of clothing with no forethought as to whether the clothes will fit into your wardrobe. Don't just buy clothes because they have had a heavy reduction. They have got to be right for you and your wardrobe. Otherwise you just waste money and go back down the road to your old cluttered, disorganised, inefficient and expensive wardrobe and will have fewer clothes that you can actually wear.

Men's capsule wardrobes are generally taken up with trousers and jeans, T- shirts and shirts and knitwear. My husband Dave, for instance, has two pairs of jeans, 4 T-shirts, three pairs of golf trousers and his golf T- shirts and probably about five navy knits which go with his T-shirts, but they are all slightly different. He has one pair of boots, one pair of deck shoes and one pair of trainers. My husband plays golf on Saturdays and Sundays and so will be seen relaxing in his golf clothes.

WHAT ACCESSORY OPTIONS ARE THERE?

"My style is not that big.
I wear heels, tight pants, and I wear diamonds."
Donatella Versace

"Fashion Changes, Style Endures"
Coco Chanel

Accessories are items which are not included in the major items of clothing but which can be used as little add-ons to add personality and style to the person's outfit. They are little touches of difference between people. Some places of work request their employees to wear a more formal style so accessories allow people to express their individuality and style.

From a gentleman's point of view accessories would include ties, cuff links shoes and socks. Choosing accessories for men is determined by their personality, preferences and the occasions they might go to. In the case of cuff links, for example, not all men like them, or would ever have the need to wear them. Each accessory item should be well-suited to the career of the man. If he was a salesman it might not be very professional if he had pictures of minions or other cartoon characters on his socks, for example. Such socks may be fine at the weekend, if he likes minions though!

Having said that the accessories are an opportunity for men to express their character and personality within the bounds of what they can do according to their career. If we look at someone like Peter Jones the entrepreneur, he is well known for having various coloured socks which may be striped, but these are always in keeping with his suits. Peter will often be seen in a navy blue suit, a smart tie co-coordinating with the shirt and the main dose of colour often comes from his socks.

When dressing casually men can also use accessories to create a different look. Shoes and socks are a good way of doing this.

Another accessory which is unisex is a wristwatch. Watches are usually personality driven and often say something about the owner. Some people have one watch for all occasions while others use them as fashion accessories.

Ladies have potentially a wider choice of accessories than do men. Jewellery accessories can include earrings, necklaces, bangles or wrist cuffs as well as wristwatches of different colours and styles.

Another popular accessory for ladies is of course the handbag. There is a whole array of possible styles with handbags, as well as choices of colours, fabrics and textures. Handbags can inject a different style. They may be angular, slouchy, colourful, fabric, leather or plastic.

Scarves, are another super accessory, they can add a different texture, colour, fabric and print to an outfit.

Shoes are a great accessory and again ladies can experiment with colours, fabrics and styles.

Accessories complete the outfit for both ladies and gentlemen. They can be used to bring the whole outfit together and to spark a bit of personality on the wearer. Imagine seeing a woman, perhaps on a weekend, wearing a black jumper with a pair of jeans. This would look quite bland. If you then added for instance a skull and cross bones scarf (if the lady was a bit of a rock chick) it would look much different. Alternatively, the same lady could add a silk Hermes style scarf to have a more classic and luxe look. An accessory can therefore be very influential in the overall style of the wearer.

Another good thing about accessories is that we can play around with them with our different outfits and experiment very easily. Furthermore, many accessories are not too pricey so we can have a little range of them.

When I am advising a lady on how many pairs of shoes she should have, we would first of all look at what shoes she needs for her wardrobe. Certainly we would look at what her lifestyle and work consisted of. If she works in an office she will need to have more formal shoes. I would then recommend having neutral tone shoes like black, navy and maybe a nude pair because she will know that these will go with anything she has in her wardrobe. The lady may want to buy shoes with a little more personality such as perhaps a leopard print, or different colour, but then she will need to be careful that it goes with the rest of her outfit. Shoes with a busy design would liven up and go with block coloured dresses or skirts. Base colour shoes will go with everything, but different colours or patterned shoes will not unless you like to print & colour clash.

In the winter season ladies often buy boots (tall, short, biker, ankle) to wear with dresses or jeans. Ladies can also buy trainers, loafers or a type of ballet pump.

All in all I recommend ladies have six pairs of shoes or boots of as high a quality as possible, but ensuring that they go with if not all of the wardrobe then most of it, so they can wear them with virtually every other item of clothing they own.

I fully appreciate that for most women the thought of only having say six pairs of shoes or boots will seem very restrictive and most of us have far more than this. It must be remembered though that less is more. If you have fewer pairs of better quality shoes you will be able to actually see them in your wardrobe and you will know that you feel good when you wear them. It is better that you get good wear out your shoes than they sit at the back of the wardrobe hardly ever seeing the light of day and then possibly not matching very well with the rest of your wardrobe. Having few items, albeit possibly of a better quality, does save money and is much less stressful.

| STEP 8 |

WHAT CLOTHES GO TOGETHER?

"Fashion is what you buy, Style is what you do with it."
Nicky Hilton

It is important to have an understanding of what clothes can go together when you create your outfit from your new wardrobe.

Starting with base neutral tones, these have a block colour so they are generally items of clothing of one colour only, and they are of a colour which goes with virtually everything else. Such block neutral tones include navy, black, a camel tone, grey and light brown. These are called 'base neutrals' and everything goes with them. Start your outfit with your base neutral tone item of clothing and then add other items of clothing knowing that they will go with them. The base neutral toned item of clothing can either be on the bottom half or the top half, or indeed a singular piece such as a dress, jumpsuit or boiler suit. If a person is wearing a mixture of base neutral tones then they can add in a print such as a floral or animal print, stripes, polka dots, tweeds and plaids. You can also look at different fabrics such as leather or denim.

For example, a person might have a pair of striped trousers on the lower half but then add in a red knit on the top half. On another day the red knit on top of would also work very well with a pair of denim jeans.

When you know that the contents of your wardrobe will interlink well then the decision is whether you go for neutral tones on the bottom or top half and then where you use prints or colours on the other half. So long as your wardrobe mixes and matches well it will work easily and simply.

The general rule of thumb is that if you have a block colour on top you have a print or colour on the bottom and vice versa. For instance, a lady could wear a really nice pair of green trousers that would provide the colour on the bottom half and then they could wear a black and white striped top.

If the same lady was wearing the block colour green trousers she could also add a really nice navy shirt that maybe has a design on it. Neutrals and prints go together.

31

But, if you are a personality that likes to really create interest to your outfit then print clashing is great too. You may choose a check with an animal print or floral with check for example.

The outfit you create must reflect your true personality, that way you will love and feel confident in what you are wearing.

From a gentleman's point of view it is possible that the majority of the time he will have block coloured trousers, pinstripe trousers or maybe a herringbone design. This allows a lot of freedom for choosing different styles of top. Generally men's prints consist of stripes predominantly, but if the man has perhaps a slightly quirky personality he might wear a floral shirt to bring colours and pastel tones, or even pinks and blues. All will go with block coloured trousers.

The clothes that don't go together are where patterns clash between the top and bottom or where the undertone of the colours don't blend well. We need to try to mix up clothes with the same colour undertone. Colour runs with what is called either a yellow undertone or it runs with a blue undertone, these being primary colours. The blue undertone colours will always complement each other because they are running with the same colour tone. Any colours with a yellow undertone will invariably complement each other because they are running with the same yellow undertone.

To work out whether clothes have a blue or yellow undertone is not always easy for people to do. For blue undertones I advise people to think about it like in seasons and flowers. If you imagine a circle and divide the circle into quarters on the right-hand side you will put the blue undertones. If you think of flowers in winter everything is quite dark and deep and every now and again you get a flash of vibrancy when the sun comes out like it is a frosty day, but it is bright. You might also have the snow where you have the icy tones. The colours in the winter flowers tend to be much deeper so might include blacks, navies, deep browns and purples. There will also be the icy colours and colours similar to the range of paints we can buy with a hint of so perhaps cerise pinks and turquoises. From a seasonal point of view winter is slightly deeper and darker.

Conversely clothes with a yellow undertone I imagine as being on the left- hand side of the circle and representing summer tones. The yellow tones are softer. Summer flowers are more pastel. Also on the left-hand side of the circle are the autumn tones which consist of oranges and slightly murky tones which when you add yellow to them they go murky such as the greens, the oranges and the chestnut browns resembling fallen leaves in autumn. The autumn tones have got far more yellow in them.

It is all about making sure that the undertone colours are identified and matched. You will find, for instance, that pale greens will not go with navy blue as they have different undertones. They do not complement each other. Conversely pale green with yellow or mustard will go beautifully together. Bear in mind that different shades of blue will have more or less yellow in them and will complement yellow more or less. A marine blue for instance will certainly go with a bright yellow tie for men. This is because a marine blue has an undertone of yellow in it whereas a navy blue does not.

Colour of clothing is a fascinating area. Men often want to understand the scientific side of understanding how colours match. Ladies are often more interested in how the colour interacts with their skin tone colouration. My *'Impact of Colour'* download is available;
https://lisatalbot.podia.com/the-impact-of-colour

CLOTHES NOT INCLUDED IN A CAPSULE WARDROBE

My style is mainly about comfort. It has to be comfortable, it has to lay right on me, know what I mean?

Ne-Yo

In the above pages I have recommended that the main items of clothing number 15 for each the two main seasons giving us a wardrobe consisting of 30 items of clothing in total. However, some items of clothing have such a specific task from a recreational point of view that they fall outside of this.

If clothes are included for when you're doing a specific recreational activity then I would not include them in the capsule wardrobe. For instance, some people enjoy gardening and they will keep a pair of gardening jeans and a top which they are happy to wear in the garden because they will get it dirty or covered in grass cuttings or clippings. These clothes would not form part of the capsule wardrobe.

Similarly people who like going to the gym or exercising will have a gym outfit. Once again this is outside the capsule wardrobe.

Many people play golf and have specific clothing to wear when they play golf. They would not go to a restaurant in that clothing. Once again golf clothing does not get included in the capsule wardrobe.

Dog owners might have dog walking clothes especially in winter because they might be going through the woods or the fields and perhaps getting muddy. These clothes wouldn't be worn at any other time in all likelihood, and so they are outside the capsule wardrobe.

Any clothing which is sport related such as tennis, badminton, squash, golf or whatever, or which do a specific job from a recreational point of view are not included in the capsule wardrobe. Work clothes, whilst intended for use in a particular job or role, are not recreational and so are included in the capsule wardrobe.

| STEP 10 |

HOW TO ORGANISE YOUR NEW WARDROBE

"Style is a reflection of your attitude and your personality."
Shawn Ashmore

By now you have removed the clothes you don't wear and trimmed down your wardrobe to have 30 items, plus accessories, plus recreational clothes for a specific job such as dog walking exercise or gardening. The next thing you need to do is to organise your clothes in your wardrobe so that you get the maximum benefit from it. There is no point having gone through all this change to then not get the most from your wardrobe.

How we organise our wardrobes is often up to us and our preferences and different people will organise their wardrobes in different ways. Some people are visually based and like to see everything clearly and laid out in a particular way. Think about what suits you best.

For instance, some clients like to organise their clothes by their colours so they will put, for instance, all their navy items of clothing together, all the red clothes together, all the pinks together and all the greens together. As a result they will have the colours together but a mixture of tops and bottoms arranged in those colours.

You can also arrange your wardrobe depending on what type of garment it is. This should mean that all of your jackets are together, as are your coats, dresses, trousers, shirts, suits, cardigans and knitwear etc.

You have a choice of two methods therefore; you can sort clothing by the type of clothing or by their colours.

You then need to decide what you will be hanging up on hangers, because not everyone hangs everything. Putting things such as knitted jumpers in drawers is fine so long as you remember what is in the drawers. Ideally a capsule wardrobe will be all together in one place as much as possible so that you can see everything and remember what you've got. If you can put everything into one place I would recommend you do that.

If you have room to hang up every item of clothing, that's fine. If you must put items of clothing in drawers then use as few drawers as possible and above all, remember what you've got in each.

I have known some people organise their wardrobes by outfit. This means that they put outfits together and hang them separately. This is not usually necessary, however, if you have a good capsule wardrobe because the vast majority of your clothes will go with everything else and so you can mix and match outfits very easily.

Another good tip is to hang your accessories on the same hanger as the clothing which they go with best. This then becomes a good prompt to know what accessories you can wear and ensures that you can find the accessories when you need them. If you have a tie which you know goes really well with a particular shirt then wrap the tie around the shirt when the shirt is being hung up. Ladies can do the same if they have different necklaces for different outfits and different garments.

Shoes should be in pairs and stored neatly and tidily. If they have to be stacked on top of each other that is fine so long as you can see them easily. Shoes can be seasonal and so as the seasons change bring that season's shoes or boots to the front of the wardrobe and put the others to the back. You don't need to see the other season's shoes for the time being so fill your view with what you will be wearing.

When organising your wardrobe take some time to think about what would work best for you and then set your wardrobe out as you would like it.

If you follow the advice I have set out above you are likely to have gone from having a fairly cluttered and possibly disorganised wardrobe into now having a beautifully laid out one with far fewer items of clothing, but far more options for different outfits. You may not be able to make this change overnight, especially if your budget does not allow you to buy new clothes right away, but stick with it. Always keep in mind your capsule wardrobe and you will save money on impulse buys that you may never wear again. You will always find it easy to find something to wear and you will always go out looking stylish and coordinated.

If you would like some help with your capsule wardrobe or with choosing what clothes would be best for you then you can contact me.

If you would like more information about the services I provide, or if you would like to discuss an aspect of this book, you can contact me as follows:-

Website: www.lisatalbot.co.uk

E-mail: info@lisatalbot.co.uk.

Instagram: lisatalbot1

Twitter: @listalbot

Facebook group: The Pocket Stylist

Facebook: Lisa-Talbot-Personal-and-Fashion- Stylist

Printed in Great Britain
by Amazon